Returning to True Worship

Calling a Generation Back to the Heart of True Worship

(John 4:24)

Marvin Marshall

i

ISBN: 978-1-969880-94-0

Dedication

To my late grandmother, Zephie Marshall—

Your quiet strength, enduring faith, and altar of prayer laid the foundation for everything I am. You taught me that worship begins in the heart and is sustained by surrender. This book is a tribute to the legacy you built in silence, sacrifice, and Spirit.

To my wife—Luanna Marshall

Your grace, wisdom, and steadfast support have carried me through every chapter of this journey. You are my anchor, my partner in purpose, and the melody behind every word. Thank you for walking with me, praying with me, encouraging me, and believing in the call.

To my children—

You are my inspiration and my legacy. May this book be a spiritual inheritance that fuels your faith, ignites your worship, and reminds you that you were born to carry the fire of God. I pray you build altars of your own and live lives of surrendered praise.

🙏 Acknowledgments

To my Lord and Savior Jesus Christ—You are the reason I sing, the One I worship, and the fire behind every word. This book is Yours.

To my wife—your grace, wisdom, and unwavering support have carried me through every chapter of this journey. You are my anchor and my inspiration.

To my children—you are my legacy. May this book be a spiritual inheritance that fuels your faith and ignites your worship.

To my grandmother, Zephie Marshall—your altar of prayer and quiet strength laid the foundation for everything I've become. This book is dedicated to your legacy.

To Pastor Hope Mc. Dowell Gibson—your prophetic voice, spiritual covering, and firm belief in me have shaped my ministry and my message. Thank you for seeing the worshiper in me.

To the No Limits Ministries International family—thank you for trusting me to lead you in worship and for walking with me through seasons of growth, refinement, and revival.

To every worship leader, pastor, and believer who longs for deeper intimacy with God—this book was written for you. May it stir your spirit, rebuild your altar, and restore your fire.

Contents

Foreword

In every generation, God calls His people back to the heart of worship. In a time when worship can easily become performance or routine, this book reminds us that true worship begins in surrender and flows from a life devoted to God.

In *Returning to True Worship: Calling a Generation Back to the Heart of True Worship*, Marvin Marshall invites readers to rediscover worship as more than music or church gatherings. Through biblical insight and spiritual reflection, he calls believers to rebuild the altar of the heart and return to worship that is rooted in Spirit and truth.

Marvin Marshall challenges us to examine our motives, deepen our relationship with God, and live lives that reflect His presence. As you read these pages, may your heart be stirred and your worship renewed.

True worship is not simply expressed in song but it is revealed in a surrendered life.

Pastor Marvin Marshall is a true worshipper whose heart for God is evident in the powerful way he leads our congregation at No Limits Ministries International into deep, intense, and Spirit-filled worship. Through his ministry, many have been drawn into a greater awareness of God's presence and a renewed passion to honor Him in spirit and in truth.

Because of the authenticity of his walk with God and his commitment to restoring reverence in the house of the Lord, I wholeheartedly recommend his book *Return to True Worship* to the entire Body of Christ. This message is both timely and necessary, calling believers back to the heart of worship and to a deeper, more intimate relationship with God.

Foreword Written By Dr Hope McDowell Gibson

Founder & President of HANS TV Network & Senior Pastor, No Limits Ministries International

Preface

Worship has always been the heartbeat of my life. Long before I held a microphone or penned a manuscript, I stood in the quiet places—lifting my voice, pouring out my heart, and encountering the presence of God. Worship was never just music to me—it was breath, fire, and surrender.

This book was birthed in those sacred spaces. In seasons of silence and storms, in moments of breakthrough and brokenness, the Lord began to stir a message in me: a call to return. Not to a style, a sound, or a system—but to the altar. To the kind of worship that moves heaven and transforms earth.

I've seen firsthand how worship can shift atmospheres, heal hearts, and restore homes. I've watched congregations awaken; families realign, and leaders reignite—not because of performance, but because of presence. And I've felt the ache of a generation longing for more than hype—longing for holiness.

This book is my offering. It's a prophetic journey through the heart of worship—from Eden's intimacy to heaven's throne room, from distortion to restoration, from personal surrender to generational legacy. It's written for worship leaders, pastors, parents, and every believer who hears the Spirit's whisper: "Come back to the altar."

I write as a worshiper first. As a husband, father, pastor, and author second. My prayer is that these pages will not only inform you—but transform you. That they will stir your spirit, challenge your rhythm, and reignite your fire.

Let's return to true worship.

Let's rebuild the altar.

Let's become the kind of worshipers the Father is seeking.

— Marvin Marshall

📖 Introduction:
The Father Is Seeking True Worshipers

"Yet a time is coming and has now come when the true worshipers will worship the Father in the Spirit and in truth, for they are the kind of worshipers the Father seeks." — John 4:23

Worship is not a genre—it's a journey. It's not confined to a sanctuary—it's cultivated in surrender. It's not just what we sing—it's how we live. And in this hour, the Father is not seeking more songs—He is seeking worshipers. True worshipers.

This book was born in a secret place. It was shaped by tears, refined by fire, and fueled by a holy hunger to see the church return to true worship. Not performance. Not routine. Not hype. But holy, Spirit-led, truth-rooted worship that pleases the Father and transforms the worshiper.

I've led worship in sanctuaries and in silence. I've sung through storms and danced through deliverance. I've seen altars rebuilt; hearts restored, and atmospheres shifted—not because of sound systems, but because of surrendered souls.

Worship is not about volume—it's about value. It's not about style—it's about Spirit.

This book is a call to return. To rebuild the altar. To restore the rhythm. To reignite the fire. It's a call to pastors, worship leaders, families, and believers who long for more. More than music. More than moments. More than mechanics. It's a call to live as the kind of worshiper the Father seeks.

We are living in a time when worship is often reduced to performance and preference. Lights, lyrics, and livestreams have replaced intimacy, reverence, and surrender. But the Spirit is stirring a remnant—a generation that longs to worship in Spirit and in Truth. A people who will not settle for emotional hype or religious habit, but who will rebuild the altar and host the presence of God.

This book is for them. For you. For every heart that has felt the ache for more. For every leader who has sensed the shift. For every believer who has whispered, "There must be more than this." You're right—there is. And it begins at the altar. You'll journey through Eden's intimacy, the distortion of worship, the restoration through Christ, and the eternal vision of heaven's throne room. You'll discover how worship becomes a lifestyle, a weapon, a legacy, and a prophetic gate. You'll be challenged to rebuild family altars, lead with purity, and live Spirit-filled.

This is not just theology—it's testimony. It's not just instruction—it's impartation. My prayer is that every chapter stirs your spirit, renews your mind, and reawakens your heart. That you'll not only understand worship—you'll embody it.

Worship is not a moment—it's a movement. It's not confined to a Sunday—it's carried into every day. It's the fire on the altar, the fragrance in the air, and the foundation beneath our feet. When we return to true worship, we return to the heart of God.

So, come. Lay down your crown. Lift up your heart. Rebuild your altar. And become the kind of worshiper the Father is seeking.

📖 Chapter 1
The Origins of Worship

"The Lord God took the man and put him in the Garden of Eden to work it and take care of it." — Genesis 2:15

"They heard the sound of the Lord God walking in the garden in the cool of the day..." — Genesis 3:8

Worship didn't begin in a temple—it began in a garden. Before there were altars, instruments, or congregations, there was intimacy. Eden was the birthplace of worship because it was the birthplace of a relationship. God walked with man, spoke with him, and invited him into communion.

Worship was not an event—it was a way of life.

🌿 Worship in Eden: Intimacy Before Instruction

In Eden, worship was not taught—it was experienced. Adam didn't need a manual to know how to respond to God's presence. He simply walked with Him. The rhythm of worship was woven into the rhythm of creation. Every breath, every step, every moment was an act of communion.

This kind of worship was pure. It wasn't filtered through fear, shame, or performance. It was unbroken fellowship. Adam didn't sing to impress—he lived to express. His worship was his work, his rest, his obedience, and his delight.

God's presence was the centerpiece of Eden. It wasn't something Adam visited—it was someone he lived with. Worship was not a destination—it was a dwelling. The garden was not just a place—it was a posture. Eden teaches us that worship is first relational, then ritual. Before there were sacrifices, there was surrender. Before there were songs, there was silence. Worship begins with proximity—being near to God, aware of Him, and responsive to Him.

This intimacy also reveals God's desire. He didn't create man to perform—He created man to partner. Worship is not about appeasing a distant deity—it's about abiding with a loving Father. Eden shows us that God's heart is for closeness, not control.

Even the work Adam was given—tending the garden—was worship. It was stewardship, obedience, and reflection of God's character. Worship is not confined to sacred spaces—it is expressed in sacred living.

When we return to Eden's model, we rediscover the simplicity of worship. It's not complicated—it's consistent. It's not loud—it's loving. It's not about doing—it's about being.

🧍 The Fall and the Fracture of Worship

But Eden didn't last. Sin entered, and worship was fractured. The moment Adam and Eve disobeyed, their intimacy was interrupted. They hid from God, covered themselves, and feared His presence. The sound that once brought joy now brought dread.

Sin distorts worship because it distorts relationship. It replaces communion with concealment. It turns worship from delight into duty. The fall didn't just break creation—it broke the rhythm of worship. God's question— "Where are you?"— was not geographical. It was relational. Worship had shifted. The altar of the heart had been compromised. Shame had silenced surrender. Fear had replaced freedom.

From that moment, worship required restoration. Altars were built, sacrifices were made, and rituals were introduced. But the goal was always the same as returning to Eden. To restore what was lost. To walk again with God in the cool of the day.

The fall also introduced false worship. Cain and Abel brought offerings—but only Abel's was accepted. Cain's worship was contaminated by comparison and control. Worship became a battleground for the heart.

This fracture reminds us that worship is vulnerable. It can be redirected, distorted, or diminished. That's why God continually calls His people back—to purity, to presence, to posture.

Even in the fall, God made a way. He covered Adam and Eve, spoke to them, and promised redemption. Worship was wounded—but not destroyed. The seed of restoration was planted.

🔥 Altars and Sacrifice: Worship Reimagined

After Eden, worship took on new forms. Altars were built to represent access to God. Sacrifices were offered to symbolize surrender. Worship became visible, tangible, and symbolic—but it was always meant to point back to intimacy.

Noah built an altar after the flood. Abraham built altars wherever he encountered God. Isaac, Jacob, and Moses followed suit. These altars were not just religious—they were relational. They marked moments of encounter, covenant, and consecration.

Sacrifice became central to worship. Blood was shed, animals were offered, and rituals were performed. These acts were not empty—they were prophetic. They pointed to the ultimate sacrifice: Jesus, the Lamb of God.

Altars also represented choice. Elijah rebuilt the altar on Mount Carmel and called Israel back to true worship. The fire fell—not because of the ritual, but because of the repentance. Worship is not about the altar's size—it's about the heart's posture. Sacrificial worship teaches us that worship costs something. It's not convenient—it's consecrated. It requires time, attention, and obedience. It's not about what we get—it's about what we give.

But even in these rituals, God's desire was intimacy. He said, "I desire mercy, not sacrifice." The altars were temporary—the relationship was eternal. Worship was never meant to be mechanical—it was meant to be meaningful.

Today, we don't build stone altars—but we build spiritual ones. We offer our bodies as living sacrifices. We lay down pride, fear, and control. We worship not with bulls and goats—but with brokenness and gratitude.

🧱 Worship as Legacy

Worship didn't end with Eden—it continued through generations. Each patriarch passed down a rhythm of worship. Abraham taught Isaac. Isaac blessed Jacob. Jacob wrestled with God and built altars. Worship became a legacy, not just a lifestyle.

Legacy worship is generational. It's not just what we do—it's what we leave behind. When we worship authentically, we create a spiritual inheritance. Our children learn to seek God, honor Him, and walk with Him—not just because we told them, but because they saw us do it.

David's worship shaped Solomon's temple. Zephie Marshall's prayers shaped Marvin's ministry. Legacy worship is powerful because it transcends time. It echoes through generations and builds altars in hearts we may never meet.

This kind of worship is intentional. It's not just emotional—it's educational. It teaches, models, and imparts. It's not just about Sunday—it's about Monday through Saturday. It's not just about music—it's about memory.

Legacy worship also requires consistency. It's not built in moments—it's built in rhythms. Daily prayer, weekly devotion, monthly reflection—these patterns create permanence. They turn worship from event into environment.

When we worship with legacy in mind, we become altar builders. We create spaces for others to encounter God. We leave behind more than songs—we leave behind surrender.

Legacy worship is also prophetic. It declares that God is worthy—not just now, but always. It says, "As for me and my house, we will serve the Lord." It builds altars that outlast us.

This is the kind of worship that changes families, churches, and nations. It's not just personal—it's generational. It's not just expressive—it's eternal.

☐ Reflection

Abraham's journey is a story of worship as a legacy. He built altars wherever he went, teaching Isaac to do the same. When God asked him to sacrifice Isaac, Abraham obeyed—not out of fear, but out of faith. His worship was costly, but it was also covenantal.

Isaac learned from his father. He dug wells and built altars. Jacob, though flawed, encountered God at Bethel and declared, "Surely the Lord is in this place." Each generation had its own encounter—but the rhythm of worship remained. This story reminds us that worship is not just about us—it's about those who follow us. Our obedience today becomes their foundation tomorrow. Our surrender becomes their strength.

📖 Chapter 2
The Distortion of Worship

"These people honor Me with their lips, but their hearts are far from Me. They worship Me in vain; their teachings are merely human rules." — Matthew 15:8–9

"Cain brought some of the fruits of the soil as an offering to the Lord... but on Cain and his offering He did not look with favor." Genesis 4:3–5

Worship is sacred—but it can be misdirected. From Cain to the Pharisees, Scripture reveals how easily worship can drift from intimacy to idolatry, from surrender to self. God desires worship that flows from the heart, not just the hands. When worship is distorted, it loses its power, purity, and purpose.

🧭 From Intimacy to Idolatry

The first distortion of worship occurred not in a pagan temple, but in a family altar. Cain and Abel both brought offerings—but only Abel's was accepted. Cain's worship was external, transactional, and self-centered. Abel's was internal, sacrificial, and Spirit-led. This moment reveals that God doesn't just receive worship—He discerns it.

Idolatry begins when worship shifts from God to self. It's not always about golden calves—it can be about pride, performance, or preference. When we worship to be seen, applauded, or validated, we've already left the altar of truth.

Cain's offering lacked heart. It was "some of the fruits"—not the first, not the best, not the surrendered. Worship that is casual becomes corrupted. God is not looking for leftovers—He's looking for lordship.

This distortion continues throughout Scripture. Israel often worshiped with their lips while chasing idols with their lives. They built altars to Baal, danced before Asherah poles, and sacrificed to false gods—all while claiming to honor Yahweh. The danger of distorted worship is that it feels spiritual but lacks substance. It may sound holy but be hollow. It may look passionate but be polluted. God sees beyond the song—He sees the source.

Idolatry also manifests in modern ways. We idolize platforms, personalities, and preferences. We chase emotional highs instead of spiritual depth. We worship itself, forgetting the One it's meant to glorify.

True worship dethrones idols. It places God at the center and removes every competing affection. It's not just about what we sing—it's about what we surrender.

To restore worship, we must confront idolatry. We must ask: Who is truly on the throne of my heart? What am I offering—and why? Is my worship about Him, or about me?

🎭 The Danger of Performance

Performance-driven worship is subtle but dangerous. It prioritizes excellence over encounter, visibility over vulnerability. It turns the altar into a stage and the sanctuary into a showroom. But God is not impressed by production—He is moved by presence. The Pharisees were masters of performance. They prayed loudly, fasted publicly, and gave visibly.

But Jesus rebuked them: "They honor Me with their lips, but their hearts are far from Me." Their worship was rehearsed, not real.

Performance worship seeks applause from men rather than approval from God. It's more concerned with optics than obedience. It asks, "Did they like it?" instead of "Was He pleased?"

This distortion often begins with good intentions. We want to serve well, sing skillfully, and lead effectively. But when excellence becomes the goal instead of the fruit, we've missed the mark. Worship is not a show—it's a sacrifice.

God desires authenticity. He wants worship that is raw, honest, and holy. He's not looking for perfection—He's looking for purity. He's not moved by technique—He's moved by truth.

Performance also creates pressure. Worship leaders feel the need to "deliver" rather than dwell. Congregants feel the need to "feel" something rather than surrender. The altar becomes a place of anxiety instead of adoration. To break the performance, we must return to the secret place. We must worship when no one is watching, sing when no one is listening, and pray when no one is applauding. That's where true worship is born.

God is not seeking performers—He's seeking worshipers. He's not looking for stars—He's looking for servants. Worship that pleases Him is not polished—it's personal.

When Worship Becomes Manipulation

Another distortion is worship as manipulation—using spiritual expression to control outcomes. This happens when we worship to "get" something from God rather than to give ourselves to Him. It turns worship into a transaction, not a transformation.

In 1 Samuel 15, Saul disobeyed God but tried to cover it with sacrifice. He said, "I did obey the Lord," while keeping the spoils of war. Samuel replied, "To obey is better than sacrifice." Saul used worship to mask rebellion.

Manipulative worship says, "If I sing loud enough, God will bless me." It treats worship like a formula, not a fellowship. It seeks results, not relationship. It's not about loving God—it's about leveraging Him. This distortion is dangerous because it feels spiritual. We may cry, lift hands, and quote Scripture—but if our hearts are not surrendered, it's empty. God cannot be bribed with praise. He desires obedience, not theatrics.

Manipulation also shows up in how we lead others. Worship leaders may push emotional responses, manufacture moments, or chase reactions. But true worship invites—not insists. It flows from the Spirit, not from strategy.

God is not moved by manipulation—He's moved by meekness. He responds to hunger, not hype. He draws near to the broken, not the boastful. Worship that pleases Him is not calculated—it's consecrated.

To confront manipulation, we must examine our motives. Why do I worship? What am I hoping to receive? Am I worshiping to move God—or to be moved by Him?

Worship is not a tool—it's a treasure. It's not a means to an end—it's the end itself. When we worship rightly, we stop trying to control God and start surrendering to Him.

Restoring the Altar of the Heart

The good news is that distorted worship can be restored. God is not looking to punish—He's looking to purify. He calls us back to the altar of the heart, where worship is reborn in intimacy, truth, and surrender.

Restoration begins with repentance. We must acknowledge where worship has drifted—into idolatry, performance, or manipulation—and return to the simplicity of devotion. God doesn't need our perfection—He desires our proximity.

The altar of the heart is built in the secret place. It's where we meet God without microphones, lights, or applause. It's where we cry, confess, and commune. It's where worship becomes real again.

This altar is also guarded. We must protect it from distraction, deception, and dilution. We must keep it holy, humble, and honest. The heart is the wellspring of worship—what flows from it shapes everything.

Restoration also requires renewal. We must renew our minds with truth, our spirits with prayer, and our habits with discipline. Worship is not just a moment—it's a mindset. It must be cultivated daily.

God is faithful to restore. He says, "Return to Me, and I will return to you." He doesn't reject the broken—He rebuilds them. He doesn't discard the distorted—He delivers them. Worship is not lost—it's waiting. When the altar of the heart is restored, worship becomes powerful again.

It breaks chains, shifts atmospheres, and pleases the Father. It becomes the kind of worship He seeks.

This restoration is not just personal—it's prophetic. It prepares the church for revival, the family for legacy, and the worshiper for eternity. It's not just about singing—it's about surrendering.

📖 Reflection

In 2 Chronicles 29, King Hezekiah reopened the temple and restored worship. The priests consecrated themselves, cleansed the sanctuary, and offered sacrifices. The people rejoiced, and the presence of God returned. Worship had been distorted—but now it was restored.

This story reminds us that revival begins with worship. When the altar is rebuilt, the fire falls. When the heart is surrendered, heaven responds. Restoration is possible—and powerful.

📖 Chapter 3
Jesus and the Restoration of Worship

"Jesus answered, 'Destroy this temple, and I will raise it again in three days.'" — John 2:19

"The hour is coming when you will neither on this mountain nor in Jerusalem worship the Father... the true worshipers will worship the Father in spirit and truth." — John 4:21–23

Jesus didn't just come to redeem sinners—He came to restore worship. His life, death, and resurrection redefined the temple, tore the veil, and reopened access to the Father. Worship was no longer confined to a place—it was released into a people. Through Christ, the altar moved from stone to soul.

🧱 The Temple Reimagined

In the Old Testament, the temple was the center of worship. It housed the Ark of the Covenant, the altar of sacrifice, and the Holy of Holies. Only priests could enter, and only the high priest could approach God once a year. Worship was sacred—but restricted.

Jesus disrupted this model. He referred to His body as the temple, declaring that true worship would no longer be tied to geography. When He died, the veil in the temple was torn from top to bottom—signaling that access to God was no longer limited. The presence of God was now available to all who believe.

This reimagining was radical. It shifted worship from ritual to relationship, from law to grace, from exclusion to inclusion. Jesus became the High Priest, the sacrifice, and the sanctuary. Through Him, we enter boldly into the presence of God.

The temple was no longer a building—it was a body. Paul writes, "Do you not know that your bodies are temples of the Holy Spirit?" Worship became mobile, personal, and perpetual. We carry the altar within us.

This shift also democratized worship. No longer was it reserved for the elite or the educated. Fishermen, tax collectors, and women became worshipers. The Samaritan woman, once marginalized, became a messenger of worship.

Jesus didn't abolish worship—He fulfilled it. He embodied every symbol, every sacrifice, every shadow. The temple pointed to Him, and in Him, worship found its true meaning.

This reimagining calls us to reverence. If we are temples, then our lives must reflect holiness. Worship is not just what we do—it's who we are. We are living sanctuaries, hosting the presence of God.

✝ The Cross as the Ultimate Altar

The cross was not just a place of death—it was a place of worship. Jesus offered Himself as the ultimate sacrifice, fulfilling every Old Testament requirement. His blood didn't just cleanse—it consecrated. The cross became the altar where heaven and earth met. Worship at the cross is raw. It confronts sin, exposes pride, and demands surrender. It's not comfortable—but it's transformative. At the cross, we see the cost of redemption and the depth of love.

Jesus didn't die to make worship easier—He died to make it eternal. His sacrifice opened a new and living way. We no longer approach God through rituals—we approach through relationship. The cross is our access point.

This altar also redefines worth. Jesus paid the highest price, declaring our value. Worship is now a response to grace, not a requirement for acceptance. We worship because we are loved—not to be loved.

The cross also silences performance. We don't earn God's presence—we receive it. Worship becomes gratitude, not guilt. It flows from freedom, not fear.

At the cross, we lay down our idols, our pride, and our control. We exchange shame for sonship, fear for faith, and striving for surrender. The cross is not just a symbol—it's a sanctuary.

This altar is also communal. Jesus died for all. Worship at the cross unites races, classes, and cultures. It levels the ground and lifts the soul. It's where we all begin again. To worship at the cross is to live crucified. It's to say, "Not my will, but Yours." It's to carry our cross daily and follow Him. This is the worship that pleases the Father.

🔥 Jesus as the Worship Leader

Jesus didn't just restore worship—He modeled it. He sang hymns, prayed often, and lived in constant communion with the Father. He didn't worship from distance—He worshiped from intimacy. He is the ultimate worship leader.

In John 17, Jesus prays for His disciples. This prayer is worship—it's intercession, surrender, and glory. He says, "I have glorified You on earth." Worship was His mission, not just His moment.

Jesus worshiped in the wilderness. After fasting for 40 days, He resisted temptation by quoting Scripture. His worship was rooted in truth, not emotion. He didn't need a crowd—He needed conviction.

He worshiped in the garden. At Gethsemane, He cried out, "Not My will, but Yours." This was worship in agony. It wasn't loud—it was loyal. It wasn't pretty—it was powerful. Worship is not always celebration—it's often consecration. Jesus also led others into worship. He taught the disciples to pray, healed the broken, and welcomed the outcast. His life was a song of surrender, a melody of mercy, and a rhythm of redemption.

As worship leader, Jesus redefined leadership. It wasn't about spotlight—it was about sacrifice. He washed feet, carried crosses, and embraced the rejected. Worship leadership is servanthood.

He also revealed the Father through worship. "If you've seen Me, you've seen the Father." Worship is revelation. It unveils God's heart, character, and kingdom. Jesus was the visible image of invisible glory.

To follow Jesus is to follow His worship. It's to live surrendered, Spirit-led, and truth-rooted. It's to glorify the Father in every word, work, and witness.

Worship as Resurrection

The resurrection was not just a miracle—it was a movement. It declared that worship is not confined to death—it flows into life. Jesus rose, and worship rose with Him. The grave could not silence the song.

Resurrection worship is victorious. It declares, "He is risen!" It celebrates triumph over sin, death, and hell. It's not mournful—it's majestic. It's not defeated—it's delivered.

This worship is also empowered. The same Spirit that raised Jesus now dwells in us. We worship with resurrection power—

bold, free, and full of authority. We are no longer slaves—we are sons.

Resurrection worship is also missional. Jesus said, "Go and make disciples." Worship leads to witness. It's not just about intimacy—it's about impact. We worship, then we walk.

This kind of worship is unstoppable. Persecution can't silence it. Prisons can't contain it. Paul and Silas sang in chains—and chains broke. Resurrection worship is revolutionary.

It also redefines suffering. We don't worship to escape pain—we worship through it. Resurrection says, "There's life after loss, joy after sorrow, and glory after grief." Worship becomes our weapon and witness.

Resurrection worship is eternal. Jesus ascended, and worship continues in heaven. Angels cry "Holy," and the redeemed cry "Worthy." We join this chorus now—and forever.

To worship in resurrection is to live risen. It's to walk in victory, speak in authority, and serve in joy. It's to declare, "I was dead—but now I live."

📖 Reflection

After the resurrection, Mary Magdalene encountered Jesus at the tomb. She didn't recognize Him at first—but when He said her name, she fell at His feet. Her worship was personal, passionate, and prophetic. She became the first witness of resurrection.

This story reminds us that worship begins with an encounter. When Jesus calls our name, we respond with surrender. Worship is not about knowing facts—it's about knowing Him.

📖 Chapter 4
Understanding Worship in Spirit and Truth

"Yet a time is coming and has now come when the true worshipers will worship the Father in the Spirit and in truth, for they are the kind of worshipers the Father seeks. God is spirit, and His worshipers must worship in the Spirit and in truth." — John 4:23–24

This passage is a turning point in the theology of worship. Spoken by Jesus to a Samaritan woman, it dismantles centuries of religious tradition and introduces a new paradigm: worship that is not bound by location, ritual, or heritage—but by Spirit and Truth. The Father is not seeking performers or ritualists—He is seeking worshipers whose hearts are aligned with heaven. This is not a suggestion; it is a divine pursuit. God is actively searching for those who will worship Him in a way that reflects His nature and His Word.

🙌 Worship as Posture, Not Performance

Worship is not a stage—it's a surrender. It's not about how loud we sing or how well we play; it's about how deeply we yield.

In a culture that often equates worship with production, God reminds us that He looks at the heart. Worship is not measured by applause but by alignment. It is the posture of a soul bowed low before a holy God.

When we reduce worship to performance, we rob it of its power. We begin to chase excellence without intimacy, visibility without vulnerability. But true worship begins in the secret place. It is cultivated in quiet moments of prayer, in whispered surrender, in unseen obedience. It is not for show—it is for Him.

The posture of worship is humility. It says, "I am not the center—You are." It dethrones ego and enthrones Christ. It silences self and magnifies the Savior. Worship is the act of placing God at the highest place in our hearts, our homes, and our habits. This posture also requires honesty. God is not impressed by masks. He desires truth in the inward parts. Worship is not pretending to be holy—it is presenting our brokenness to the One who makes us whole. It is the place where we stop hiding and start healing.

Worship as posture means we come as we are—but we don't stay as we are. In His presence, we are transformed. We are refined by His fire, renewed by His Spirit, and redirected by His Word. Worship is not static—it is sanctifying.

When we worship from posture, not performance, we become vessels of encounter. We host His presence, not just His praise. We carry His glory, not just His gifting. We become altars, not just artists.

This kind of worship is what the Father seeks. Not just sound—but surrender. Not just excellence—but essence. Worship that flows from posture will always reach heaven.

☐ Spirit and Truth as Twin Pillars

Jesus didn't say worship must be in Spirit *or* Truth—He said *both*. These are the twin pillars that uphold authentic worship. Spirit without Truth leads to emotionalism; Truth without Spirit leads to legalism. Together, they create a foundation that is both passionate and pure.

To worship in Spirit means to be led by the Holy Spirit. It is dynamic, intimate, and alive. The Spirit stirs our affections, aligns our desires, and empowers our expressions. He reveals the heart of the Father and draws us into deeper communion. Spirit-led worship is not confined to a setlist—it flows with the wind of heaven.

To worship in Truth means to be anchored in Scripture. It is informed, reverent, and rooted. Truth protects worship from error and manipulation. It ensures that our songs reflect sound doctrine and our hearts reflect biblical conviction. Truth is not restrictive—it is liberating.

These pillars also reflect God's nature. He is Spirit—eternal, invisible, omnipresent. And He is Truth—unchanging, faithful, righteous. When we worship in Spirit and Truth, we are aligning with who He is. We are not creating worship—we are responding to revelation.

Spirit and Truth also shape our identity as worshipers. The Spirit reminds us we are sons and daughters; Truth reminds us we are servants and stewards. The Spirit draws us close; Truth keeps us grounded. Together, they form worshipers who are both intimate and obedient. This balance is essential in today's church. We must resist the temptation to chase emotional highs without theological depth—or to cling to doctrine without spiritual fire. The Father is seeking worshipers who carry both—who burn with passion and walk in purity.

When Spirit and Truth converge, worship becomes transformative. It doesn't just move the room—it moves the heart. It doesn't just stir emotions—it sanctifies lives. It becomes the kind of worship that heaven recognizes, and the Father receives.

🧡 The Kind of Worship God Seeks

God is not seeking worship—He is seeking worshipers. This distinction is vital. Worship is not an event to be attended or a sound to be produced; it is the overflow of a life surrendered. The Father is not impressed by volume, style, or stage presence. He is moved by hearts that are humble, honest, and hungry for Him.

In John 4:23, Jesus says the Father is actively seeking true worshipers. This implies that not all worship is received. Some worship is self-centered, performance-driven, or disconnected from truth. But true worship—the kind God desires—is marked by Spirit and Truth. It is both intimate and informed, passionate, and pure.

God seeks worship that flows from relationship, not routine. He desires worship that is birthed in the secret place, not just the sanctuary. The kind of worship He seeks is not confined to Sunday mornings—it permeates every moment of our lives. It is expressed in how we speak, serve, give, and live.

This worship is sacrificial. It costs something. David said, "I will not offer the Lord that which costs me nothing." True worship requires time, attention, repentance, and obedience. It is not convenient—it is consecrated. It is not casual—it is covenantal.

God seeks worship that is Spirit-led. This means we are sensitive to His presence, responsive to His promptings, and surrendered to His will. Spirit-led worship is not about hype— it's about holiness. It's not about emotionalism—it's about an encounter. It flows from a heart that is yielded and a life that is aligned.

He also seeks worship that is rooted in Truth. This means our worship is anchored in Scripture, shaped by sound doctrine, and reflective of God's character. Truth protects worship from error and manipulation. It ensures that our songs match our theology and our hearts match His Word.

The kind of worship God seeks is also consistent. It doesn't fluctuate with feelings or circumstances. It remains steady in the storm, faithful in the valley, and fervent on the mountaintop. It is not seasonal—it is steadfast. It is not situational—it is spiritual.

This worship is also reverent. It honors God's holiness, respects His majesty, and acknowledges His sovereignty. It is not flippant or familiar—it is filled with awe. Reverence doesn't mean rigidity—it means recognition. We recognize who He is, and we respond accordingly.

God seeks worship that is transformative. It doesn't just stir emotions—it sanctifies lives. It doesn't just move the room—it moves the heart. True worship changes us. It convicts, cleanses, and commissions. It draws us near and sends us out.

Ultimately, the kind of worship God seeks is the kind that reflects His nature. He is Spirit—so we worship in Spirit. He is Truth—so we worship in Truth. He is holy—so we worship in holiness. He is love—so we worship in surrender. This is the worship that pleases the Father and transforms the worshiper.

📖 Reflection

One of the most powerful examples of worship in Spirit and Truth is found in Luke 7. A sinful woman enters a Pharisee's house, breaks an alabaster jar, and pours perfume on Jesus' feet. She weeps, wipes His feet with her hair, and kisses them. The religious leaders are offended—but Jesus is moved.

Her worship was not rehearsed—it was raw. It was not polished—it was prophetic. She didn't come with a song—she came with surrender. She worshiped in Spirit, led by love and brokenness. And she worshiped in Truth, recognizing who Jesus was and what He deserved.

Jesus said, "She has loved much." Her worship was costly, intimate, and pure. It wasn't about her reputation—it was about His worth. She didn't care who was watching—she only cared that He was present.

This story reminds us that true worship is not about perfection—it's about passion. It's not about being clean—it's about being close. It's not about being seen—it's about seeing Him rightly. Her worship changed the atmosphere. It silenced critics, shifted hearts, and drew the attention of heaven. That's what happens when we worship in Spirit and Truth.

📖 Chapter 5
Worship as a Lifestyle

"Therefore, I urge you, brothers and sisters, in view of God's mercy, to offer your bodies as a living sacrifice, holy and pleasing to God—this is your true and proper worship." — Romans 12:1

Paul's exhortation reframes worship from an event to an existence. It's not just about what we do in church—it's about how we live in Christ. Worship is not confined to a moment; it's expressed in every movement, decision, and devotion. It's not just a song—it's a sacrifice.

🏠 Worship Beyond the Sanctuary

Worship doesn't end when the music fades—it begins when we walk out the door. True worship is lived in the mundane, the messy, and the meaningful. It's how we treat others, steward our time, and respond to trials. The sanctuary may inspire us—but the lifestyle reveals us.

In Scripture, worship was never limited to temples. Abraham worshiped on mountains, David in caves, Paul in prisons. Their lives were altars, and their obedience was incense. Worship is not about location—it's about devotion.

When worship becomes a lifestyle, it permeates everything. We worship when we forgive, when we serve, when we sacrifice. We worship when we choose integrity over convenience, purity over popularity, and surrender over control.

This kind of worship is consistent. It doesn't depend on feelings or circumstances. It remains steady in storms and faithful in valleys. It's not seasonal—it's spiritual. It's not reactive—it's rooted.

Lifestyle worship also transforms the environment. A worshipful heart shifts atmospheres at work, at home, and in community. It brings peace to chaos, light to darkness, and grace to brokenness. Worship is contagious when it's authentic.

It also requires intentionality. We must choose to worship daily—not just emotionally, but practically. It's setting our minds on things above, renewing our thoughts, and aligning our actions. Worship is not passive—it's purposeful.

This kind of worship pleases God. It's not just about what we say—it's about how we live. It's not just about Sunday—it's about Monday through Saturday. Worship becomes our witness.

When we live worshipfully, we become walking sanctuaries. Our lives echo heaven's rhythm. Our choices reflect God's character. Our presence becomes prophetic.

🔥 Living Sacrifices

Paul's call to offer our bodies as living sacrifices is radical. In the Old Testament, sacrifices were dead—slain on altars. But in Christ, we are called to live surrendered. Our worship is not in dying once—it's in dying daily.

Living sacrifices are active. They choose obedience over comfort, holiness over habit, and surrender over self. They climb onto the altar willingly, knowing that fire refines and presence purifies.

This kind of worship is costly. It requires letting go of pride, plans, and preferences. It's saying, "Not my will, but Yours." It's trusting God with our time, talents, and treasures. It's not convenient—it's consecrated.

Living sacrifices also reflect Christ. He offered Himself fully—body, soul, and spirit. He didn't hold back. He didn't negotiate. He laid down His life in love. Our worship mirrors His. This surrender is not weakness—it's worship. It's strength under submission, power under purpose. It's choosing to be holy, not just happy. It's choosing to be faithful, not just fruitful. Living sacrifices also require renewal. Paul says, "Be transformed by the renewing of your mind." Worship begins in thought before it flows into action. We must align our thinking with truth, our emotions with grace, and our habits with holiness.

This kind of worship is pleasing to God. It's not just expressive—it's obedient. It's not just passionate—it's pure. It's not just loud—it's loyal.

To be a living sacrifice is to live crucified. It's to carry our cross daily, to die to self, and to live for Christ. It's not glamorous—but it's glorious.

Worship in Work, Rest, and Relationships

Worship as a lifestyle touches every area of life—including work, rest, and relationships. It's not compartmentalized—it's comprehensive. Every task becomes sacred when done unto the Lord.

Work becomes worship when we serve with excellence, integrity, and humility. Whether we're leading teams or cleaning floors, we reflect God's character. Colossians 3:23 says, "Whatever you do, work at it with all your heart, as working for the Lord."

Rest becomes worship when we honor Sabbath, embrace stillness, and trust God with our pace. In a culture of hustle, rest is prophetic. It declares, "God is my source, not my striving." Worship includes silence, solitude, and sabbath.

Relationships become worship when we love sacrificially, forgive freely, and honor consistently. Marriage, friendship, and community are altars where God's presence dwells. When we treat others with grace, we reflect His glory.

This integration requires awareness. We must see every moment as an opportunity to worship. Every conversation, decision, and interaction becomes a chance to glorify God.

It also requires discipline. Worship is not automatic—it's cultivated. We must guard our hearts, steward our time, and prioritize presence. Worship is not just spontaneous—it's structured.

When worship flows into every area, life becomes liturgy. We don't just sing songs—we live them. We don't just attend services—we become servants. Worship becomes our rhythm. This kind of worship is holistic. It doesn't separate sacred from secular. It sees all of life as spiritual. It's not just about what happens in church—it's about what happens in character.

Worship as Witness

When worship becomes a lifestyle, it becomes a witness. People see our surrender, hear our praise, and feel our peace. Worship is not just vertical—it's visible. It reveals God to the world.

Jesus said, "Let your light shine before others, that they may see your good deeds and glorify your Father in heaven." Worship is light. It's not hidden—it's holy. It draws others to the altar.

Worship as witness is powerful. It speaks louder than sermons and sings deeper than songs. It's how we live, love, and lead. It's how we respond to trials, treat enemies, and serve strangers.

This witness is prophetic. It declares that God is real, present, and powerful. It says, "I've been changed—and you can be too." It's not about perfection—it's about presence.

Worship also breaks barriers. It transcends culture, language, and denomination. It unites believers and invites seekers. It's not exclusive—it's expansive.

To worship as witness is to live evangelistically. It's to carry the gospel in our actions, attitudes, and atmosphere. It's to be salt and light, fragrance and fire.

This kind of worship is missional. It doesn't stay in the sanctuary—it moves into the streets. It doesn't stay in the heart—it flows into the hands. Worship becomes service.

When people encounter worshipers who live surrendered, they encounter God. Our lives become altars, our homes become sanctuaries, and our presence becomes prophetic.

Worship as witness is legacy. It's what we leave behind. It's how we're remembered. It's how heaven is revealed on earth.

📖 Reflection

In Acts 16, Paul and Silas were beaten and imprisoned. Yet at midnight, they sang hymns. Their worship wasn't circumstantial—it was spiritual. The prison shook, chains fell, and doors opened. Their worship became a witness.

The jailer, moved by their praise, asked, "What must I do to be saved?" Worship led to salvation. This story reminds us that worship is not just for God—it's for others. It's not just vertical—it's viral.

From Lifestyle to Language

When worship becomes a lifestyle, praise and thanksgiving become its language. These aren't just expressions—they're spiritual strategies. Let's uncover how praise breaks chains and thanksgiving build resilience.

📖 Chapter 6
The Power of Praise and Thanksgiving

"Enter His gates with thanksgiving and His courts with praise; give thanks to Him and praise His name." — Psalm 100:4

"About midnight Paul and Silas were praying and singing hymns to God... and suddenly there was a violent earthquake..." — Acts 16:25–26

Praise and thanksgiving are not just expressions—they are spiritual strategies. They open gates, shift atmospheres, and release breakthrough. When worship becomes a lifestyle, praise and thanksgiving become its language. They are not optional— they are essential.

🎶 Praise as a Weapon

Praise is not passive—it's powerful. It's not just a response to victory—it's a catalyst for it. In Scripture, praise often preceded breakthrough. Jehoshaphat sent worshipers ahead of the army. As they sang, God ambushed their enemies. Praise confused the enemy and confirmed God's presence.

Praise shifts our focus. It lifts our eyes from problems to promises, from fear to faith. It magnifies God and minimizes anxiety. When we praise, we declare that God is bigger than our battle, stronger than our storm, and faithful in every season.

Praise also silences the enemy. Psalm 8:2 says, "Through the praise of children and infants You have established a stronghold... to silence the foe." Praise is spiritual warfare. It dismantles lies, breaks chains, and releases truth.

In Acts 16, Paul and Silas were beaten and imprisoned. Yet at midnight, they sang. Their praise wasn't circumstantial—it was spiritual. The prison shook, chains fell, and doors opened. Praise didn't follow the miracle—it caused it. This kind of praise is sacrificial. It's not based on feelings—it's based on faith. It's choosing to sing in the storm, to shout in the valley, and to declare God's goodness when nothing looks good.

Praise also invites presence. God inhabits the praises of His people. When we praise, we create a throne for Him to sit on. We host heaven in our hearts, homes, and gatherings.

Praise is prophetic. It declares what God has said, even when we haven't seen it yet. It speaks into the future with confidence, not fear. It's not just celebration—it's declaration.

To wield praise as a weapon is to fight with faith. It's to resist despair, reject defeat, and release victory. It's not just noise— it's authority.

🏛 Thanksgiving as a Posture

Thanksgiving is more than gratitude—it's a posture of the heart. It acknowledges God's goodness, even in difficulty. It says, "I may not understand—but I trust." It's not just polite—it's powerful. In Psalm 100, we're told to enter God's gates with thanksgiving. This implies that gratitude is the doorway to deeper worship. Without thanksgiving, we remain outside. With it, we step into His courts.

Thanksgiving also builds resilience. It reminds us of what God has done, which strengthens us for what He will do. It shifts our perspective from lack to abundance, from complaint to contentment.

This posture is protective. Philippians 4:6−7 says, "Do not be anxious... but in every situation, by prayer and petition, with thanksgiving, present your requests to God." Thanksgiving guards our hearts and minds with peace.

Gratitude also cultivates humility. It acknowledges that every good gift comes from above. It dethrones entitlement and enthrones appreciation. It says, "I didn't earn this—I received it."

Thanksgiving is also contagious. When we live gratefully, we inspire others to do the same. Our posture becomes a witness. Our peace becomes prophetic.

This posture must be practiced. Gratitude is not automatic—it's intentional. We must choose to see, remember, and respond. Journaling, prayer, and reflection help cultivate this rhythm.

Thanksgiving also honors God. It tells Him, "I see Your hand, I trust Your heart, and I thank You for both." It's not just a response—it's a revelation.

To live in thanksgiving is to live in worship. It's to walk through life with open eyes, open hands, and an open heart.

🧱 Praise and Thanksgiving in the Valley

The true test of praise and thanksgiving is not on the mountaintop—it's in the valley. It's easy to sing when things are good. But when life is hard, praise becomes a sacrifice. Thanksgiving becomes a discipline.

David wrote many psalms from caves, not castles. His praise was raw, honest, and holy. He said, "I will bless the Lord at all times." Not just in triumph—but in trouble. His worship was not circumstantial—it was covenantal.

In the valley, praise becomes prophetic. It declares what we believe, not just what we see. It says, "God is good—even here." It's not denial—it's defiance. It defies despair and declares hope.

Thanksgiving in the valley is also healing. It shifts our focus from pain to presence. It reminds us that God is near, even when life feels far. It's not just emotional—it's spiritual.

This kind of worship requires maturity. It's not about hype—it's about holiness. It's not about feeling—it's about faith. It's choosing to worship when it hurts, to thank when it's hard, and to praise when it's painful.

Praise and thanksgiving in the valley also release breakthrough. They open prison doors, parted Red Seas, and silenced lions. They don't just comfort—they conquer.

This worship is also intimate. God draws near to the brokenhearted. He doesn't reject our tears—He receives them. Our valley worship becomes incense in His throne room.

To worship in the valley is to trust God's character over our circumstances. It's to say, "Even if You don't deliver me—I will still worship You." That's the kind of worship that moves heaven.

🧱 The Language of Heaven

Praise and thanksgiving are not just earthly expressions— they are heavenly languages. In Revelation, angels cry "Holy," and the redeemed cry "Worthy." Heaven is not silent—it sings. It praises. It thanks.

When we worship with praise and thanksgiving, we join heaven's chorus. We echo eternity. We align with the rhythm of the throne room. Our worship becomes timeless.

This language also transcends culture. Every tribe, tongue, and nation will worship. Praise and thanksgiving unite believers across boundaries. They are universal expressions of divine encounter.

Heaven's language is also pure. It's not tainted by pride, performance, or preference. It's holy, humble, and honest. It flows from revelation, not routine.

When we adopt heaven's language, we shift atmospheres. Our homes become sanctuaries. Our churches become portals. Our hearts become altars.

This language also prepares us for eternity. Worship is the one activity we do now that continues forever. Praise and thanksgiving are not just preparation—they are participation.

Heaven's language is also powerful. It releases healing, deliverance, and joy. It's not just poetic—it's prophetic. It speaks life into death, light into darkness, and hope into despair.

To speak heaven's language is to live heaven's reality. It's to walk in victory, dwell in presence, and overflow with glory.

Praise and thanksgiving are not just tools—they are truths. They are not just expressions—they are encounters. They are the language of heaven—and the lifestyle of the redeemed.

📖 Reflection

In Luke 17, ten lepers were healed—but only one returned to thank Jesus. He fell at His feet, praising God. Jesus asked, "Where are the other nine?" Gratitude mattered. Praise mattered. The thankful leper was not just healed—he was made whole.

This story reminds us that thanksgiving completes the miracle. Praise seals the breakthrough. Worship is not just about receiving—it's about returning.

📖 Chapter 7
The Role of the Church in Worship

"Let the word of Christ dwell in you richly... teaching and admonishing one another with all wisdom through psalms, hymns, and songs from the Spirit, singing to God with gratitude in your hearts." — Colossians 3:16

"Where two or three gather in My name, there am I with them." — Matthew 18:20

Worship was never meant to be solo. From the tabernacle to the temple, from the upper room to the modern sanctuary, God has always called His people to worship together. The church is not just a building—it's a body. And when the body worships in unity, heaven responds.

🏛 Worship as Community

Worship in the church is communal. It's the gathering of believers to exalt God, encourage one another, and encounter His presence. It's not just about personal devotion—it's about corporate declaration. When we worship together, we amplify the sound of surrender.

The early church understood this. In Acts 2, they met daily, broke bread, and worshiped with glad hearts. Their unity created momentum. Their praise attracted presence. Their worship was not just vertical—it was visible.

Community worship also reflects heaven. Revelation describes multitudes from every tribe and tongue worshiping before the throne. The church is a rehearsal for eternity. It's where we learn to harmonize our hearts with heaven's rhythm.

This kind of worship requires humility. We lay down preferences, styles, and egos to exalt one name. We sing with others, not over them. We listen, respond, and participate. Worship becomes a shared offering. Corporate worship also strengthens faith. When we're weak, others lift us. When we're silent, others sing. The sound of the church becomes a shelter, a sanctuary, and a source of strength. We don't worship alone— we worship together.

Community worship also teaches us accountability. We're reminded that our lives affect others. Our worship is not isolated—it's interconnected. We carry one another's burdens, celebrate one another's victories, and grow together.

This worship is also prophetic. It declares unity in a divided world, peace in a chaotic culture, and hope in a hurting generation. The church becomes a beacon of light through its worship.

To worship in community is to reflect the heart of God. He is relational, communal, and covenantal. He dwells among His people—not just within individuals.

🎤 Worship Leadership and Stewardship

Worship in the church requires leadership—but not just musical. It requires spiritual stewardship. Worship leaders are not performers—they are priests. They host presence, discern flow, and protect purity. In the Old Testament, Levites were set apart to minister before the Lord. Their role was sacred. They didn't just sing—they served. They didn't just play—they prayed. Worship leadership was about consecration, not charisma.

Today, worship leaders must carry that same weight. They are gatekeepers of the altar, stewards of the sound, and shepherds of the moment. Their role is not to entertain—it's to encounter.

This leadership requires preparation. Not just rehearsals— but prayer. Not just planning—but presence. Worship leaders must be filled before they pour. They must be hidden before they're highlighted.

Stewardship also means protecting the atmosphere. Leaders must guard against distraction, division, and distortion. They must cultivate reverence, unity, and authenticity. The altar must remain holy.

Worship leadership is also pastoral. It's about guiding people into God's presence, not just guiding them through a setlist. It's about sensing the Spirit, responding to needs, and releasing truth.

This role is not glamorous—it's glorious. It's not about spotlight—it's about sacrifice. Worship leaders must be servants first, singers second. Stewardship also includes mentoring. Leaders must raise up others, not just raise volume. They must disciple, develop, and delegate. Worship is generational.

To lead worship is to lead hearts. It's to carry the weight of glory, the burden of purity, and the joy of surrender. It's not just a role—it's a responsibility.

Worship and Unity in the Body

Worship in the church is a unifier. It brings together diverse people under one name. It transcends race, age, background, and denomination. It says, "We may be different—but He is the same."

Unity in worship is powerful. Psalm 133 says, "Where there is unity, God commands a blessing." When the church worships in harmony, heaven responds with favor, fire, and fullness.

This unity requires intentionality. We must choose love over preference, grace over offense, and humility over pride. Worship is not about style—it's about spirit. It's not about genre—it's about Jesus. Unity also reflects the Trinity. Father,

Son, and Spirit—three in one. Our worship mirrors divine relationship. It becomes a dance of diversity and a chorus of covenant.

Disunity disrupts worship. Offense, division, and comparison silence the sound. We must guard the altar from gossip, jealousy, and competition. The church must be a place of peace.

Unity in worship also heals. It brings reconciliation, restoration, and renewal. It breaks walls, builds bridges, and binds wounds. Worship becomes a balm.

This unity is not uniformity. We don't all look the same—but we all lift the same name. We bring our uniqueness to the altar and find common ground in Christ.

To worship in unity is to declare, "We are one body, one Spirit, one hope." It's to reflect heaven on earth. It's to become the bride, not just the building.

🧱 The Church as a Worship Movement

The church is not just a worship service—it's a worship movement. It's a living, breathing body that carries the sound of heaven into the streets. Worship doesn't stop at the sanctuary—it spills into society.

This movement is missional. It sends worshipers into workplaces, schools, and neighborhoods. It equips believers to carry presence, release praise, and live surrendered. Worship becomes a witness.

The church as a worship movement is prophetic. It declares truth in culture, hope in crisis, and light in darkness. It doesn't just sing—it speaks. It doesn't just gather—it goes.

This movement is also creative. It births songs, art, dance, and declarations. It reflects the Creator through creativity. Worship becomes expression, innovation, and inspiration.

The church must embrace this identity. It's not just a place—it's a people. It's not just a program—it's a presence. Worship is not confined—it's commissioned.

This movement also requires mobilization. Leaders must activate worshipers, not just audiences. They must release gifts, empower voices, and cultivate calling. Worship becomes a lifestyle of impact.

The church as a worship movement is unstoppable. Persecution can't silence it. Politics can't control it. Culture can't contain it. It's Spirit-led, truth-rooted, and glory-driven.

To be part of this movement is to live missionally, worship prophetically, and serve sacrificially. It's to say, "We are the church—and we will worship."

📖 Reflection

In 2 Chronicles 5, the priests and Levites gathered in unity. They sang, "He is good; His love endures forever." The glory of the Lord filled the temple so powerfully that the priests couldn't stand to minister. Worship in unity released glory. This story reminds us that when the church worships together, heaven responds. Glory falls. Presence dwells. Lives change. Worship is not just sound—it's surrender.

📖 Chapter 8
Returning to the Altar

"Elijah repaired the altar of the Lord that had been torn down... Then the fire of the Lord fell and burned up the sacrifice..." — 1 Kings 18:30, 38

"Present your bodies as a living sacrifice, holy and acceptable to God..." — Romans 12:1

Before fire falls, the altar must be rebuilt. In every generation, God calls His people back to the place of consecration, surrender, and encounter. The altar is not just a symbol—it's a strategy. It's where heaven meets earth and where worship becomes warfare.

🧱 The Significance of the Altar

The altar is one of the most sacred spaces in Scripture. It's where sacrifices were made, covenants were sealed, and encounters with God occurred. From Noah to Abraham, Moses to Elijah, the altar was central to worship. It wasn't just a place—it was a posture.

Altars represented access. They were built to honor God, to seek Him, and to respond to His voice. They marked moments of revelation, repentance, and renewal. They were physical expressions of spiritual surrender.

In Elijah's day, the altar had been torn down. Israel had turned to Baal, and worship was distorted. Elijah's first act wasn't to call down fire—it was to rebuild the altar. Restoration always begins with repentance. Revival always begins with return.

The altar also represents intimacy. It's where we meet God—not just with words, but with sacrifice. It's where we lay down pride, fear, and control. It's where we say, "Not my will, but Yours."

Today, the altar is not made of stone—it's made of surrender. It's the place in our hearts where we yield to God. It's the space in our homes where we seek Him. It's the rhythm in our lives where we honor Him.

Rebuilding the altar means restoring priority. It means putting God first again—in time, thought, and trust. It means removing idols, distractions, and compromises. It's not just about emotion—it's about obedience.

The altar is also a place of fire. When it's rebuilt, God responds. His presence comes, His power is released, and His glory is revealed. But the fire doesn't fall on empty altars—it falls on sacrifice.

To return to the altar is to return to the heart of worship. It's to say, "Here I am, Lord—consume me." It's to live consecrated, committed, and connected.

🔥 Rebuilding the Altar in Our Lives

Rebuilding the altar is personal. It starts with us. It's not about waiting for revival—it's about becoming it. We must examine our hearts, our habits, and our homes. Where have we drifted? What needs to be restored? This rebuilding requires honesty. We must confront compromise, confess sin, and commit to change. The altar is not a place of shame—it's a place of grace. God doesn't expose to condemn—He exposes to heal.

It also requires intentionality. We must carve out time, create space, and cultivate rhythm. The altar is built in consistency. Daily prayer, Scripture, and surrender become the bricks of devotion.

Rebuilding the altar means restoring reverence. We must treat God as holy, not casual. We must honor His presence, not just enjoy it. Worship is not entertainment—it's encounter.

This process is also painful. Sacrifice hurts. Surrender costs. But the reward is worth it. When the altar is rebuilt, peace returns, power flows, and purpose is clarified.

We must also rebuild the altar in our homes. Family worship, shared prayer, and spiritual conversation create legacy. The altar becomes generational. Children learn to seek God—not just in church, but in the living room. Rebuilding the altar in our churches means prioritizing presence over performance. It means creating space for God to move, not just for people to be impressed. It means restoring purity, passion, and prophetic flow. This rebuilding is not a one-time event—it's a lifestyle. The altar must be maintained, guarded, and honored. It's not just about fire—it's about faithfulness.

🧍 Elijah's Example: Confrontation and Consecration

Elijah's story on Mount Carmel is a blueprint for altar restoration. He confronted idolatry, called for decision, and rebuilt the altar. His worship was not passive—it was prophetic. It challenged culture and called down heaven. Elijah didn't start with fire—he started with foundation. He repaired what was broken. He used twelve stones to represent unity. He dug a trench, prepared the sacrifice, and soaked it with water. His worship was deliberate, detailed, and devoted.

This example teaches us that worship requires preparation. We must be intentional, not impulsive. We must build with care, not convenience. The altar must be holy.

Elijah also confronted false worship. He asked, "How long will you waver between two opinions?" Worship demands decision. We cannot serve two masters. We must choose whom we will worship. His consecration was complete. He didn't hold back. He didn't compromise. He didn't negotiate. He offered everything—and God responded with fire.

This fire was not just symbolic—it was supernatural. It consumed the sacrifice, the stones, the water, and the dust. It left no doubt—God was present. Worship that is pure releases power that is undeniable.

Elijah's example also reminds us that worship is warfare. He stood alone against hundreds of prophets. He didn't flinch. He didn't fold. He worshiped with boldness.

To follow Elijah's example is to rebuild, repent, and release. It's to confront idols, consecrate altars, and call down fire. It's to live surrendered and see heaven respond.

🧱 The Altar as a Place of Identity

The altar is not just where we meet God—it's where we discover ourselves. It's where identity is affirmed, destiny is revealed, and calling is clarified. When we worship, we are reminded of who we are and whose we are.

In Genesis 22, Abraham built an altar to sacrifice Isaac. But in that moment, God revealed Himself as Jehovah Jireh—and reaffirmed Abraham's faith. The altar became a place of revelation and identity. Worship clarifies identity. It silences lies, breaks shame, and releases truth. It says, "You are loved, chosen, and called." It replaces fear with faith and confusion with clarity. The altar also affirms calling. Isaiah saw the Lord and cried, "Woe is me." But after the altar encounter, he said, "Here am I—send me." Worship commissions us. It doesn't just comfort—it calls.

This place is also healing. Brokenness is met with mercy. Regret is met with redemption. The altar becomes a place of restoration. We leave changed.

Identity is not found in performance—it's found in presence. The altar strips away titles, roles, and masks. It reveals the true self—loved by God, called by grace, and empowered by the Spirit.

To return to the altar is to return to identity. It's to say, "I am Yours." It's to receive affirmation, alignment, and assignment. Worship becomes the mirror of heaven.

This identity is not fragile—it's fortified. It's built on truth, sealed by grace, and sustained by presence. The altar becomes our anchor.

When we know who we are, we worship differently. We worship boldly, freely, and faithfully. We worship not to earn— but to express. We worship from identity, not insecurity.

📖 Reflection

In Genesis 28, Jacob encountered God at Bethel. He saw a ladder reaching heaven and heard God's voice. He built an altar and said, "Surely the Lord is in this place." That moment changed him. He went from deceiver to worshiper, from wanderer to covenant carrier.

This story reminds us that the altar is transformative. It's where we meet God—and where we meet ourselves. Worship is not just revelation—it's redefinition.

📖 Chapter 9
Worship in Spirit-Filled Living

"Do not get drunk on wine, which leads to debauchery. Instead, be filled with the Spirit, speaking to one another with psalms, hymns, and songs from the Spirit." — Ephesians 5:18–19

"God is spirit, and His worshipers must worship in the Spirit and in truth." — John 4:24

Worship without the Holy Spirit is like a lamp without oil. It may look bright for a moment, but it cannot sustain the flame. Spirit-filled living is not optional for the worshiper—it is essential. The Spirit empowers, purifies, and sustains worship that pleases the Father.

🔥 The Role of the Holy Spirit in Worship

The Holy Spirit is the breath of worship. He stirs our affections, aligns our desires, and empowers our expressions. Without Him, worship becomes mechanical. With Him, it becomes miraculous. He is not an accessory to worship—He is the essence of it.

In Scripture, the Spirit hovered over the waters, filled the tabernacle, and descended at Pentecost. He is the presence of

God made manifest. When we worship in Spirit, we are not just singing—we are communing. We are engaging with the living God.

The Spirit also convicts. He reveals areas of pride, sin, and distraction. He doesn't condemn—He cleanses. Worship becomes a refining fire, not just a feel-good moment. We are purified in His presence.

He also comforts. In seasons of grief, loss, or confusion, the Spirit ministers peace. Worship becomes a balm, a refuge, and a reminder. We are not alone—we are accompanied. Spirit-led worship is dynamic. It flows with spontaneity, sensitivity, and surrender. It may break the script, shift the atmosphere, or silence the room. The Spirit leads—not the schedule.

This kind of worship requires discernment. We must listen, respond, and yield. The Spirit is gentle but powerful. He doesn't force—He invites. Worship becomes a dance, not a duty.

The Spirit also empowers gifts. Prophetic songs, healing declarations, and spiritual language flow from Spirit-filled worship. It's not just expressive—it's explosive. Heaven touches earth.

To worship in Spirit is to worship in fullness. It's to be led, filled, and transformed. It's not just emotional—it's eternal.

🕊 Living a Spirit-Filled Life

Spirit-filled worship flows from Spirit-filled living. We cannot compartmentalize the Spirit to Sunday mornings. He must dwell in our decisions, our disciplines, and our daily rhythms. Worship is not just an event—it's an existence.

Living Spirit-filled means being continually filled—not just occasionally touched. Paul says, "Be filled with the Spirit"—present tense, ongoing. It's not a one-time encounter—it's a lifestyle of surrender.

This life is marked by fruit. Love, joy, peace, patience, kindness, goodness, faithfulness, gentleness, and self-control. These are not just virtues—they are worship. They reflect the character of Christ.

Spirit-filled living also requires intimacy. We must cultivate relationship, not just rely on power. The Spirit is a person—not a force. He speaks, leads, and loves. We must know Him.

It also requires obedience. The Spirit leads us into truth, holiness, and mission. We cannot worship in Spirit and live in rebellion. Worship must be matched by walk.

This life is also supernatural. We are empowered to witness, serve, and overcome. We are not limited by flesh—we are led by fire. Worship becomes warfare, and life becomes liturgy.

Spirit-filled living is also countercultural. It resists pride, performance, and pressure. It embraces humility, holiness, and hope. It's not trendy—it's transformative.

To live Spirit-filled is to live surrendered. It's to say, "Fill me, lead me, use me." It's to walk in step with heaven and reflect the heart of God.

Barriers to Spirit-Filled Worship

Many believers struggle to worship in Spirit because of internal barriers. Fear, pride, distraction, and unbelief can hinder flow. The Spirit is willing—but we must be open.

Fear says, "What will people think?" Pride says, "I've got this." Distraction says, "I'm too busy." Unbelief says, "Is this real?" These voices silence surrender. They block breakthrough.

To overcome these barriers, we must renew our minds. We must replace lies with truth, shame with grace, and hesitation with hunger. Worship begins in thought before it flows into expression.

We must also cultivate hunger. The Spirit fills the hungry, not the hurried. We must make room, create space, and prioritize presence. Worship is not rushed—it's reverent. Community helps. Spirit-filled worship thrives in unity. When we gather with others who are hungry, we are stirred, strengthened, and stretched. Iron sharpens iron.

We must also confront control. The Spirit cannot be managed—He must be yielded to. Worship is not about maintaining image—it's about releasing intimacy. We must let go.

Sin must be confessed. The Spirit is holy. He dwells in purity. Worship that is Spirit-filled must be Spirit-cleansed. Repentance is not shame—it's surrender.

To remove barriers is to rebuild the altar. It's to say, "Come, Holy Spirit." It's to invite, receive, and respond. Worship becomes a river—not a ritual.

Spirit-Filled Worship as Revival

Spirit-filled worship is not just personal—it's prophetic. It releases revival. When the church worships in Spirit and Truth, heaven responds with power, presence, and transformation.

Revival begins at the altar. It's not about crowds—it's about consecration. When hearts are surrendered, the Spirit moves. Worship becomes the spark. In Acts 2, the Spirit fell—and worship erupted. Tongues, prophecy, and praise filled the room. Thousands were saved. The church was born. Worship was the catalyst.

Spirit-filled worship breaks chains. It heals bodies, restores minds, and revives souls. It's not just emotional—it's explosive. It shifts cities, not just services.

This revival is sustainable. It's not hype—it's holiness. It's not momentary—it's missional. Spirit-filled worship leads to Spirit-filled living, which leads to Spirit-filled legacy.

Revival also purifies. It exposes sin, confronts idols, and restores truth. Worship becomes a mirror and a fire. It doesn't just comfort—it convicts.

This worship is also inclusive. Sons, daughters, old, young—all are filled. The Spirit is poured out on all flesh. Worship becomes generational.

To worship in Spirit is to prepare for revival. It's to say, "Let Your kingdom come." It's to host heaven, release glory, and walk in power.

Spirit-filled worship is not a style—it's a surrender. It's not a sound—it's a spark. It's the beginning of awakening.

📖 Reflection

In Acts 2, the disciples were gathered in one place. Suddenly, a sound like a rushing wind filled the room. Tongues of fire rested on each of them. They began to worship in languages they didn't know. The Spirit fell—and revival began.

This story reminds us that Spirit-filled worship is catalytic. It births movements, transforms lives, and glorifies God. It's not just for the upper room—it's for every room.

📖 Chapter 10
The Eternal Worship of Heaven

"Day and night they never stop saying: 'Holy, holy, holy is the Lord God Almighty, who was, and is, and is to come.'" — Revelation 4:8

"Then I heard every creature in heaven and on earth and under the earth and on the sea... saying: 'To Him who sits on the throne and to the Lamb be praise and honor and glory and power, forever and ever!'" — Revelation 5:13

Heaven is not silent—it sings. Worship is not just an earthly expression—it is an eternal reality. From angels to elders, from redeemed saints to creation itself, heaven resounds with praise. To understand worship fully, we must lift our eyes and catch a glimpse of eternity.

👑 The Throne Room of Worship

In Revelation 4, John is caught up into heaven and sees a throne. Around it are twenty-four elders, four living creatures, and countless angels. The atmosphere is electric with worship. There is no distraction, division, or delay—only devotion.

The throne is central. Worship in heaven is not about us—it's about Him. Everything revolves around the One seated in glory. The elders cast their crowns, the creatures cry "Holy," and the angels declare His worth. Worship is not optional—it's instinctive.

This throne room reveals the nature of God. He is holy, eternal, and sovereign. Worship is the response to revelation. The more we see Him, the more we surrender. Heaven's worship is not forced—it's fueled by awe.

The throne also represents authority. Worship acknowledges God's rule, reign, and righteousness. It dethrones idols and enthrones Christ. In heaven, there is no competition—only coronation.

This worship is continuous. Day and night, without ceasing, heaven declares His glory. There are no breaks, no boredom, no burnout. Worship is the rhythm of eternity.

The throne room also reveals order. Each being has a role, a sound, and a posture. Worship is not chaotic—it's coordinated. It's not random—it's reverent.

To worship like heaven is to center our lives around the throne. It's to cast our crowns, cry "Holy," and live surrendered. It's to make God the focus, not just the feature.

This vision calls us higher. It invites us to align our earthly worship with heavenly reality. It's not just inspiration—it's instruction.

🎶 The Sound of Heaven

Heaven has a sound. It's not just noise—it's glory. It's the roar of praise, the whisper of holiness, and the symphony of surrender. Revelation describes thunder, harps, and voices like rushing waters. Worship in heaven is immersive.

This sound is diverse. Every tribe, tongue, and nation joins the chorus. Worship is not limited by language—it's liberated by love. Heaven celebrates unity in diversity.

The sound is also layered. Angels sing "Holy," the redeemed cry "Worthy," and creation echoes praise. Each voice adds depth, dimension, and devotion. Worship is not solo—it's symphonic.

Heaven's sound is pure. There is no pride, performance, or pretense. It flows from truth, intimacy, and revelation. It's not rehearsed—it's real.

This sound is also responsive. It reacts to revelation, responds to glory, and reverberates with surrender. Worship is not static—it's alive.

The sound of heaven is contagious. When we hear it, we are changed. It stirs hunger, breaks chains, and ignites fire. It's not just heard—it's felt.

This sound also shapes culture. Earthly worship that echoes heaven transforms atmospheres. It brings healing, hope, and holiness. Worship becomes a portal. To carry heaven's sound is to carry heaven's heart. It's to sing with angels, cry with elders, and roar with creation. It's to release eternity into time.

This sound is our inheritance. We were made to worship. Our voices were designed for glory. Heaven's sound is not distant—it's destined.

The Role of the Redeemed

In Revelation 5, the Lamb takes the scroll—and worship erupts. The elders fall down, the angels sing, and the redeemed declare, "Worthy is the Lamb!" This moment reveals the unique role of the redeemed in eternal worship.

Angels cry "Holy"—but only the redeemed cry "Worthy." We worship from experience, not just observation. We've been saved, sealed, and sanctified. Our worship is personal.

The redeemed carry testimony. We've been delivered from darkness, healed from brokenness, and restored to purpose. Our worship is not just theological—it's transformational.

This worship is also eternal. We will worship forever—not out of obligation, but out of overflow. Gratitude fuels glory. Love fuels loyalty.

The redeemed also carry authority. We are kings and priests, seated with Christ, clothed in righteousness. Our worship is not timid—it's triumphant.

This role is also relational. We are sons and daughters, not just servants. We worship as family, not just followers. The Father delights in our praise.

The redeemed worship with memory. We remember the cross, the resurrection, and the redemption. Our songs are soaked in testimony.

This worship is also missional. It declares the gospel, invites the lost, and glorifies the Lamb. It's not just vertical—it's viral.

To worship as the redeemed is to worship with fire. It's to declare, "I was lost—but now I'm found." It's to sing from scars, shout from surrender, and praise from promise.

This role is sacred. We are the only ones who can sing this song. Angels marvel—but we magnify. Heaven waits for our voice.

Preparing for Eternal Worship

Eternal worship begins now. We don't wait for heaven to worship—we align with heaven on earth. Every song, surrender, and sacrifice prepares us for eternity.

Preparation requires perspective. We must lift our eyes from temporary to timeless. Worship is not just about now—it's about forever. It's rehearsal for glory.

It also requires purity. Heaven's worship is holy. We must cleanse our hearts, renew our minds, and consecrate our lives. Worship is not casual—it's consecrated.

Preparation includes practice. Daily devotion, corporate praise, and sacrificial living tune our hearts. We learn to worship in Spirit and Truth.

This preparation is also prophetic. It declares, "Your kingdom come." Worship invites heaven into earth, eternity into time, and glory into grit. We must also prepare with passion. Heaven is not bored—it's burning. Worship is fervent, focused, and free. We must stir hunger, not just habit.

Preparation includes posture. We must bow low, lift hands, and open hearts. Worship is embodied. It's physical, emotional, and spiritual.

This preparation is communal. We worship with others, not just alone. The church becomes a choir, a covenant, and a catalyst.

To prepare for eternal worship is to live surrendered. It's to say, "I'm ready." It's to echo heaven, exalt Christ, and embrace glory.

This preparation is joyful. We don't dread eternity—we delight in it. Worship becomes our joy, our journey, and our jubilee.

📖 Reflection

In Revelation 7, John sees a great multitude worshiping before the throne. They wear white robes, hold palm branches, and cry, "Salvation belongs to our God!" These are the redeemed—worshiping with passion, purity, and purpose.

This story reminds us that worship is our destiny. It's not just what we do—it's who we are. Heaven is waiting for our voice.

📖 Chapter 11
Eternal Worship (Expanded Vision)

"After this I looked, and there before me was a great multitude that no one could count... standing before the throne and before the Lamb. They were wearing white robes and were holding palm branches in their hands." — Revelation 7:9

"They sang a new song, saying: 'You are worthy to take the scroll and to open its seals, because You were slain, and with Your blood You purchased for God persons from every tribe and language and people and nation.'" — Revelation 5:9

Eternal worship is not just a future reality—it's a present invitation. Heaven's vision of worship is expansive, inclusive, and prophetic.

It reveals the heart of God and the destiny of the redeemed. To expand our vision of worship is to align with eternity.

🌍 Worship for Every Tribe and Tongue

Heaven's worship is multicultural, multiethnic, and multilingual. Revelation 7 shows a multitude from every tribe, tongue, and nation worshiping together. This is not symbolic—it's strategic. God's heart is for all people.

This vision challenges exclusivity. Worship is not reserved for one style, one culture, or one denomination. It's a global chorus. Every voice matters. Every sound belongs. The diversity of worship reflects the creativity of God.

It also affirms dignity. Every person, regardless of background, is invited to the throne. Worship is not about status—it's about surrender. The Lamb was slain for all. This vision also confronts division. Racism, elitism, and tribalism have no place at the altar. Worship unites what the world divides. It becomes a prophetic declaration of reconciliation.

Multicultural worship is not chaotic—it's coordinated. Each voice adds depth, dimension, and devotion. The Spirit harmonizes hearts across languages and lands.

This worship is also healing. It restores identity, affirms belonging, and releases joy. It says, "You are seen, known, and loved." Worship becomes a balm for brokenness.

To embrace this vision is to expand our sound. It's to welcome songs from other cultures, rhythms from other lands, and expressions from other generations. Worship becomes a mosaic.

This vision also prepares us for eternity. If we're going to worship together forever, we must start now. The church becomes a rehearsal for heaven.

The Song of the Redeemed

In Revelation 5, the redeemed sing a new song. It's not just poetic—it's prophetic. It declares the worth of the Lamb and the power of His blood. This song is unique to those who've been saved.

Angels cry "Holy"—but only the redeemed cry "Worthy." We worship from experience, not just observation. Our song carries testimony, tears, and triumph.

This song is new—not recycled. It flows from fresh revelation, renewed gratitude, and restored identity. Worship is not stale—it's Spirit-breathed.

The song of the redeemed is also powerful. It shifts atmospheres, silences shame, and releases glory. It's not just melody—it's ministry.

This song is personal. It reflects our journey, our healing, and our hope. It's not just corporate—it's intimate. Each voice carries a story.

It's also communal. Though personal, it's shared. The redeemed sing together, declaring one message: "Worthy is the Lamb." Worship becomes a covenant.

This song is eternal. It doesn't fade—it flourishes. It's not bound by time—it's birthed in eternity. We will sing it forever.

To sing this song is to live surrendered. It's to declare, "I've been purchased, purified, and positioned." Worship becomes our witness.

This song is also missional. It invites others to join the chorus. It says, "Come and see." Worship becomes evangelism.

🔥 The Glory of the Lamb

At the center of eternal worship is the Lamb. Not just the throne—but the sacrifice. Revelation reveals Jesus as both Lion and Lamb. Worship is not just about power—it's about redemption.

The Lamb is worthy because He was slain. His blood purchased us. His sacrifice redeemed us. Worship flows from the cross to the crown.

This glory is not distant—it's intimate. The Lamb bears scars. He remembers suffering. He welcomes worshipers with mercy, not judgment.

Worship of the Lamb is reverent. It's not casual—it's consecrated. We fall down, cast crowns, and cry out. We recognize the cost.

This worship is also victorious. The Lamb triumphed over death, hell, and the grave. Our praise is not mournful—it's majestic. We worship from victory.

The Lamb's glory is inclusive. He purchased people from every background. Worship becomes a celebration of grace.

This glory also transforms. As we behold the Lamb, we become like Him. Worship sanctifies, purifies, and commissions. It's not just adoration—it's activation.

To worship the Lamb is to worship with fire. It's to declare, "You are worthy." It's to live in awe, walk in surrender, and sing with passion.

This worship is eternal. It never ends, never fades, never fails. The Lamb is forever worthy—and we are forever worshipers.

Living with Heaven in View

To expand our vision of eternal worship is to live with heaven in view. It's to let eternity shape our priorities, our praise, and our purpose. Worship becomes our compass. Living with heaven in view means choosing to surrender rather than striving. It means remembering that we are pilgrims, not settlers. Worship keeps us anchored in hope.

It also means living holy. Heaven is pure. Our worship must reflect that. We pursue righteousness, resist compromise, and embrace consecration.

This perspective brings peace. When life is hard, worship lifts our eyes. It reminds us that glory is coming, that pain is passing, and that joy is eternal.

Living with heaven in view also fuels mission. We worship—but we also witness. We invite others to the throne. Worship becomes invitation.

It shapes our gatherings. Church becomes rehearsal, not routine. We sing with passion, pray with power, and serve with joy. Worship becomes prophetic.

This vision also sustains us. When we feel weary, worship revives. When we feel lost, worship leads. Heaven's sound becomes our strength.

To live with heaven in view is to live with purpose. It's to say, "I was made to worship—and I will worship forever." It's to align earth with eternity. This perspective is not escapism—it's empowerment. It doesn't ignore reality—it infuses it with glory. Worship becomes our lens.

📖 Reflection

In Revelation 21, John sees a new heaven and a new earth. The old has passed away. God dwells with His people. There is no more death, mourning, or pain. Worship is unhindered, uninterrupted, and unending.

This story reminds us that worship is our destiny. It's not just what we do—it's who we are. Heaven is not just a place—it's a posture.

📖 Chapter 12
Worship and Warfare

"After consulting the people, Jehoshaphat appointed men to sing to the Lord and to praise Him for the splendor of His holiness... As they began to sing and praise, the Lord set ambushes against the men of Ammon and Moab..." — 2 Chronicles 20:21–22

"The weapons we fight with are not the weapons of the world. On the contrary, they have divine power to demolish strongholds." — 2 Corinthians 10:4

Worship is not just adoration—it's activation. It's not just intimacy—it's intercession. In the spiritual realm, worship is a weapon. It shifts atmospheres, silences enemies, and releases victory. When we worship, we engage in warfare.

⚔️ Worship as a Weapon

Worship is one of the most underestimated weapons in the believer's arsenal. It doesn't look like a sword or a shield—but it pierces darkness and defends truth. When we worship, we declare God's sovereignty over every situation.

Jehoshaphat's story is a blueprint. Faced with overwhelming odds, he didn't send soldiers—he sent singers. As they praised,

God ambushed their enemies. Worship didn't follow the victory—it caused it.

This weapon works because it shifts focus. Instead of magnifying the problem, we magnify the Lord. Instead of reacting in fear, we respond in faith. Worship realigns our perspective and releases heaven's strategy.

Worship also silences the enemy. Psalm 8:2 says, "Through the praise of children... You silence the foe." The enemy thrives on noise—fear, accusation, distraction. Worship quiets the chaos and amplifies truth.

It also invites presence. God inhabits praise. When He shows up, enemies scatter. Worship becomes a throne for the King—and where the King reigns, victory is assured.

This weapon is accessible. You don't need a platform—just a posture. You don't need a microphone—just a mouth. Worship can be whispered, shouted, sung, or spoken. It's not about volume—it's about authority.

Worship also breaks chains. Paul and Silas sang in prison—and the earth shook. Chains fell, doors opened, and lives were changed. Worship doesn't just comfort—it liberates.

To wield worship as a weapon is to fight with faith. It's to declare, "God is greater." It's to resist despair, reject defeat, and release deliverance.

Worship in the Midst of Battle

Worship is not reserved for victory—it's required in battle. It's easy to praise after breakthrough—but powerful to praise before it. Worship in warfare is prophetic. It declares what God will do, even when we haven't seen it yet.

David understood this. Surrounded by enemies, he wrote, "I will bless the Lord at all times." His worship was not circumstantial—it was covenantal. He didn't wait for peace—he praised in pressure.

This kind of worship is sacrificial. It costs something. It's not convenient—it's consecrated. It's choosing to lift hands when you feel heavy, to sing when you feel silent, to declare when you feel defeated.

Worship in battle also builds resilience. It strengthens the soul, steadies the heart, and stabilizes the mind. It's not just emotional—it's spiritual. It anchors us in truth.

It also releases strategy. In 2 Kings 3, Elisha said, "Bring me a harpist." As the music played, the word of the Lord came. Worship creates clarity. It opens ears and aligns hearts.

This worship is also communal. When the church worships in battle, unity is forged. We fight together, sing together, and stand together. Worship becomes a shield. It's also prophetic. It declares victory before it's visible. It says, "God is faithful," even when the outcome is uncertain. Worship becomes a declaration of trust.

To worship in battle is to resist fear. It's to say, "I will not be moved." It's to stand firm, sing loud, and surrender fully. Worship becomes our warfare.

🧱 Worship and Spiritual Authority

Worship is not just emotional—it's governmental. It releases spiritual authority. When we worship, we exercise dominion. We declare God's rule over our lives, our homes, and our regions.

Jesus said, "All authority in heaven and on earth has been given to Me." When we worship Him, we align with that authority. We become ambassadors of heaven.

This authority is not loud—it's legal. It's not about hype— it's about holiness. Worship is a legal transaction. It dethrones darkness and enthrones Christ.

Worship also releases prophetic authority. Songs become swords. Declarations become decrees. Praise becomes proclamation. We speak what heaven is saying.

This authority is also territorial. Worship shifts regions. It breaks strongholds, releases revival, and establishes righteousness. Cities change when churches worship.

It's also generational. Worship releases legacy. It breaks curses, restores families, and ignites inheritance. Authority flows through worship.

To walk in spiritual authority, we must walk in purity. The enemy is not afraid of noise—he's afraid of holiness. Worship must be clean to be powerful.

This authority is also relational. It flows from intimacy. The closer we are to the throne, the greater our authority. Worship is not just warfare—it's proximity.

To worship with authority is to declare, "Thy kingdom come." It's to release heaven into earth, truth into lies, and light into darkness.

Worship as Intercession

Worship is not just praise—it's prayer. It's intercession wrapped in melody, surrender wrapped in sound. When we worship, we stand in the gap. We become bridges between heaven and earth.

In Exodus 17, Moses lifted his hands while Joshua fought. As long as his hands were raised, Israel prevailed. Worship is intercession. It sustains the battle.

This intercession is powerful. It shifts atmospheres, breaks barriers, and releases breakthrough. It's not passive—it's prophetic. Worship becomes warfare on behalf of others.

It's also personal. We intercede for family, friends, and nations. Our worship becomes a cry, a call, and a covering. We sing for those who cannot.

Worship as intercession is Spirit-led. The Spirit groans through us. Songs become sighs, melodies become movements. We pray in tongues, in tears, and in truth.

This worship is also strategic. It targets strongholds, releases healing, and declares destiny. It's not random—it's revelatory.

Intercessory worship is also persistent. It doesn't stop until breakthrough comes. It presses in, pushes through, and prevails. Worship becomes travail.

It's also communal. Worship teams become prayer teams. Congregations become battalions. The church becomes a house of prayer.

To worship as intercession is to love deeply. It's to carry burdens, release hope, and declare freedom. Worship becomes compassion in action.

This intercession is eternal. Jesus ever lives to intercede. When we worship, we join Him. We echo heaven's heart.

📖 Reflection

In Exodus 15, after crossing the Red Sea, Moses and Miriam led Israel in worship. They sang, "The Lord is my strength and my defense; He has become my salvation." Their worship was not just celebration—it was warfare. It declared victory, silenced fear, and honored God.

This story reminds us that worship is a response to deliverance—and a weapon for future battles.

📖 Chapter 13
The Worship Leader's Heart

"Man looks at the outward appearance, but the Lord looks at the heart." — 1 Samuel 16:7

"Create in me a clean heart, O God, and renew a right spirit within me." — Psalm 51:10

Before the worship leader lifts a microphone, they must lift their heart. Before they lead a congregation, they must be led by the Spirit. The heart of the worship leader is the altar from which all ministry flows. It must be pure, surrendered, and Spirit-filled.

❤️ Character Before Charisma

In a culture that celebrates talent, God still prioritizes character. The worship leader's voice may move a room—but it's their heart that moves heaven. Charisma may attract crowds, but character sustains calling.

David was chosen not because of his appearance, but because of his heart. He was a shepherd, not a showman. He worshiped in fields before he ever led in courts. His songs were birthed in solitude, not spotlight.

Character is built in a secret place. It's forged in prayer, refined in obedience, and revealed in testing. The worship leader must cultivate integrity, humility, and holiness—not just skill.

This character is also consistent. It doesn't fluctuate with applause or affirmation. It remains steady in silence and faithful in obscurity. It's not reactive—it's rooted.

Character also protects the platform. It guards against pride, comparison, and compromise. It ensures that the altar remains holy, and the ministry remains pure. The worship leader must be teachable. They must welcome correction, pursue growth, and embrace accountability. Character is not perfection—it's progression.

This heart must also be compassionate. Worship is not just vertical—it's pastoral. The leader must love people, not just lead songs. They must see beyond performance to presence.

To lead with character is to lead with credibility. It's to say, "Follow me as I follow Christ." It's to model surrender, not just sound.

🔥 The Call to Consecration

Consecration is the foundation of worship leadership. It's the setting apart of the heart, the sanctifying of the life, and the surrendering of the will. The worship leader is not just a musician—they are a minister.

In the Old Testament, Levites were consecrated for worship. They didn't just rehearse—they repented. They didn't just perform—they purified. Their role was sacred.

Today, worship leaders must carry that same weight. They must live holy, walk humbly, and serve faithfully. Consecration is not legalism—it's love. It's saying, "I'm Yours."

This consecration affects every area—speech, conduct, relationships, and rhythms. It's not just about Sunday—it's about Monday through Saturday. The altar must be maintained.

Consecration also requires boundaries. The worship leader must guard their heart, steward their time, and protect their purity. Not everything is permissible—not everything is beneficial.

It's also about posture. Consecration says, "Not my will, but Yours." It lays down ego, ambition, and agenda. It embraces servanthood over stardom.

This call is costly. It may mean saying no to opportunities, platforms, or relationships. But the reward is presence. Consecration invites glory.

The consecrated heart is sensitive to the Spirit. It discerns flow, responds to prompting, and hosts heaven. Worship becomes encounter.

To be consecrated is to be commissioned. It's to carry fire, release fragrance, and reflect the Father. Worship becomes more than music—it becomes ministry.

🧱 The Weight of Responsibility

Worship leadership carries weight. It's not just about leading songs—it's about leading souls. The worship leader sets the spiritual tone, cultivates atmosphere, and hosts presence. This is not a light task.

Responsibility begins with preparation. Not just musical— but spiritual. The leader must pray, study, and seek. They must be filled before they pour.

It also includes discernment. The worship leader must sense what God is doing, where He's leading, and how He's moving. They must be flexible, not formulaic.

This weight includes stewardship. The leader must steward their gift, their team, and their influence. They must lead with integrity, not insecurity.

Responsibility also means modeling. The worship leader is watched—on and off stage. Their life must reflect their lyrics. Their walk must match their worship.

It includes mentoring. Worship leaders must raise up others, not just raise volume. They must disciple, develop, and delegate. Legacy matters.

This weight is not burdensome—it's beautiful. It's the privilege of partnering with heaven, of leading people into encounter, of glorifying God.

But it must be carried with grace. The worship leader must rest, recharge, and receive. Burnout is real—but avoidable. Sabbath is sacred.

To carry this weight is to walk in wisdom. It's to say, "Lord, I'm available." It's to lead with love, serve with joy, and worship with fire.

🧱 The Heart That Hosts Heaven

The worship leader's heart is a sanctuary. It's where heaven dwells, where glory rests, and where fire burns. To host heaven is to cultivate purity, intimacy, and expectancy.

This heart is tender. It weeps in worship, rejoices in surrender, and trembles in awe. It's not hardened by routine— it's softened by revelation.

It's also hungry. It longs for more of God, more of His presence, more of His power. It's not satisfied with performance—it pursues an encounter.

The heart that hosts heaven is humble. It doesn't seek spotlight—it seeks surrender. It says, "He must increase—I must decrease."

It's also holy. It resists compromise, embraces conviction, and pursues consecration. It's not perfect—but it's pure.

This heart is responsive. It listens to the Spirit, follows His lead, and yields to His flow. Worship becomes a dance, not a duty.

It's also prophetic. It sings what heaven is saying, declares what God is doing, and releases what the Spirit is stirring. Worship becomes revelation.

The heart that hosts heaven is also healed. It's been touched by grace, restored by mercy, and renewed by love. It worships from wholeness.

To host heaven is to honor God. It's to say, "This is Your space." It's to create room, cultivate reverence, and carry glory.

This heart is rare—but it's required. Worship leadership begins here. Not with sound—but with surrender.

☐ Reflection

In 1 Samuel 16, David is chosen as king—not because of his appearance, but because of his heart. He was a worshiper before he was a warrior, a shepherd before he was a sovereign. His songs shaped his soul. His heart hosted heaven. This story reminds us that God chooses worship leaders based on heart, not hype. He looks for purity, not performance.

📖 Chapter 14
Building Family Altars

"As for me and my house, we will serve the Lord." — Joshua 24:15

"Isaac built an altar there and called on the name of the Lord. There he pitched his tent, and there his servants dug a well." — Genesis 26:25

The altar is not just for the sanctuary—it belongs in the home. Family altars are sacred spaces of worship, prayer, and legacy. They are places where generations meet God, where homes become holy ground, and where spiritual rhythm is restored.

🏠 The Altar as a Place of Encounter

In Scripture, altars were built wherever God was encountered. Abraham built altars in the wilderness. Isaac built them near wells. Jacob built them after dreams. These altars marked moments of divine visitation—and they became memorials for generations.

In the home, the altar is not made of stone—it's made of surrender. It's the place where families gather to pray, worship, and seek God together. It's where children learn to hear His voice, and parents model His presence.

This altar is not confined to a room—it's cultivated in rhythm. It's the morning devotion, the evening prayer, and the spontaneous praise. It's the intentional setting aside of time to honor God.

Family altars restore spiritual order. They dethrone distraction and enthrone devotion. They shift the atmosphere from chaos to peace, from noise to nearness.

They also create legacy. Children remember the prayers of their parents, the songs of their siblings, and the presence that filled the room. These memories become anchors in adulthood.

The altar is also a place of healing. Families bring their burdens, confess their faults, and receive grace. It becomes a space of reconciliation and renewal.

This encounter is not forced—it's invited. The altar is not about pressure—it's about presence. It's not about perfection—it's about pursuit.

To build a family altar is to declare, "God dwells here." It's to make the home a sanctuary, the living room a tabernacle, and the kitchen table a communion space.

🧱 Generational Worship and Legacy

Worship is generational. What we model today will become a memory tomorrow. The songs we sing, the Scriptures we read, and the prayers we pray echo through time. Family altars are legacy builders. Abraham passed worship to Isaac. Isaac passed it to Jacob. Jacob passed it to Joseph.

Each generation had its own encounter—but the rhythm was inherited. Worship became a generational thread.

Legacy worship is intentional. It's not just about what we do—it's about what we leave. It's teaching children to seek God, not just to attend church. It's modeling surrender, not just singing songs.

This legacy is also prophetic. It declares, "As for me and my house..." It sets a spiritual trajectory. It builds altars that outlast us.

Generational worship requires consistency. It's not built in moments—it's built in rhythms. Daily devotion, weekly reflection, and seasonal consecration create permanence.

It also requires vulnerability. Parents must share testimonies, confess struggles, and model repentance. Worship becomes authentic.

Legacy worship is also communal. It includes grandparents, siblings, and spiritual mentors. The altar becomes a family affair. This worship is not just vertical—it's horizontal. It strengthens relationships, restores unity, and releases blessing. The altar becomes a place of covenant.

To build legacy is to build altars. It's to say, "We will worship—not just now, but always." It's to create spiritual inheritance.

🔥 Restoring the Rhythm of the Home

Many homes have lost their rhythm. Busyness, entertainment, and distraction have replaced devotion. The altar has been neglected. But God is calling families back—to rhythm, to reverence, to restoration.

Restoring rhythm begins with priority. Worship must be scheduled, not squeezed. It must be central, not supplemental. The altar must be rebuilt.

It also requires simplicity. Family worship doesn't need to be elaborate. A Scripture, a song, a prayer—it's enough. The goal is presence, not performance. Rhythm is also relational. It's not just about God—it's about each other. Worship becomes a bonding moment. It heals wounds, deepens connection, and fosters unity.

This restoration requires leadership. Parents must lead. They must initiate, inspire, and intercede. The altar is built by example.

It also requires flexibility. Rhythm may shift—but the heart remains. Worship can happen in the car, at the table, or during bedtime. The altar is mobile.

Restoring rhythm also brings peace. It calms anxiety, silences fear, and releases joy. The home becomes a haven.

This rhythm is prophetic. It declares, "God is welcome here." It invites angels, releases glory, and hosts heaven.

To restore rhythm is to restore reverence. It's to say, "This house belongs to the Lord." It's to make worship a lifestyle, not just a liturgy.

🧱 The Family Altar as a Prophetic Gate

The family altar is not just a place of devotion—it's a gate of intercession. It becomes a portal through which heaven touches earth, and generations are shaped by glory.

This gate is spiritual. It releases protection, provision, and prophetic insight. It becomes a watchtower over the home.

It's also missional. Families pray for neighbors, nations, and needs. The altar becomes a launchpad for ministry.

This gate is generational. Parents bless children, children honor parents, and legacy is sealed. Worship becomes a covenant.

It's also territorial. The altar claims the home for Christ. It resists darkness, releases light and establishes authority.

This gate is active. It's not just symbolic—it's strategic. Families declare Scripture, release praise, and host presence. Worship becomes warfare.

It's also restorative. Broken homes are healed, prodigals are called back, and marriages are renewed. The altar becomes a place of miracles.

To build this gate is to build legacy. It's to say, "This house is holy ground." It's to invite God to dwell, to reign, and to restore. This altar is not optional—it's essential. It's the heartbeat of the home, the foundation of faith, and the gateway to glory.

📖 Reflection

In Genesis 26, Isaac built an altar, pitched his tent, and dug a well. Worship, dwelling, and provision were linked. His altar became a generational marker. His son Jacob would later return to that place and encounter God.

This story reminds us that family altars are not just for today—they are for tomorrow. They become wells of worship for generations to draw from.

📖 Conclusion

From the Altar to the Throne: Living as a True Worshiper

🧭 A Journey of Return

We began this journey with a simple yet profound truth: the Father is seeking worshipers who will worship in Spirit and in Truth. Along the way, we've walked through Eden's intimacy, humanity's distortion, Christ's restoration, and the eternal vision of worship that awaits us in glory.

We've seen that worship is not confined to a song or a service—it is a lifestyle. It is the posture of the heart, the rhythm of the home, the sound of the church, and the language of heaven. It is both a weapon in warfare and a wellspring of wonder. It is the altar we build, the legacy we leave, and the fire we carry. This is more than a book—it's a call. A call to return. To rebuild. To realign. To remember. To reignite. It's a call to become the kind of worshiper the Father seeks.

🕊 A Final Charge

Worshiper, you are not just a singer—you are a sanctuary. You are not just a voice—you are a vessel. You are not just a participant—you are a priest. You carry the presence of God.

Let your life be an altar. Let your home be a sanctuary. Let your worship be a witness. Let your heart burn with holy fire. Let your voice echo heaven.

Whether you are a pastor, a parent, a worship leader, or a new believer—this call is for you. Return to the altar. Rebuild what's been broken. Restore what's been lost. And release what's been buried.

The world doesn't need more performers—it needs more priests. It doesn't need louder songs—it needs deeper surrender. It doesn't need more light—it needs more life. You were made to worship. You were redeemed to worship. You will worship forever. So, begin now. Live as a true worshiper.

🙏 Closing Prayer

Heavenly Father,

We come before You with hearts bowed low and hands lifted high.
We thank You for the journey—through Eden, through the cross,
through the altar, and into Your throne room.
We repent for where we've drifted, performed, or forgotten.
We return to You with all our hearts.
Make us true worshipers.
Worshipers in Spirit and in Truth.
Worshipers who live surrendered, walk consecrated, and sing with
fire.
Worshipers who build altars in our homes, our churches, and our
hearts.
We lay down our crowns.
We cast off distraction, pride, and fear.
We say, "Here we are, Lord—send us."
Let our lives be incense. Let our homes be sanctuaries. Let our worship
be a witness.
We long for Your glory.
We wait for Your fire.
We welcome Your presence.
And we declare: You are worthy.
Forever and ever, Amen.

About the Author

Marvin Marshall is a Praise and Worship Pastor, author, and prophetic voice committed to restoring authentic worship in the body of Christ. With a ministry rooted in Spirit-led living and legacy-building, Marvin has served in diverse roles—from pastor and worship leader to flight attendant and manager—but his heart has always been anchored in worship.

He is the author of

Returning to True Worship,

Weathering the Storms and

Awaken Your Greatness

and leads worship at No Limits Ministries International in Mississauga, Ontario. Marvin's writing blends theological insight with emotional resonance, calling believers to rebuild personal and family altars, embrace Spirit-filled living, and prepare for eternal worship.

For Marvin, family is his greatest joy and inspiration. His life and ministry are dedicated to honoring the legacy of his grandmother, Zephie Marshall, and to equipping worshipers to live surrendered, Spirit-led lives.